Karin Walker is the founder of KGW Family Law, a niche family law practice based in Woking. A former Chair of Resolution's national DR Committee (2014-2017), Karin has always been keen to promote out of court dispute resolution. Her aim is to assist clients settle issues on separation through constructive communication.

A Family Lawyer, Mediator, Collaborative Practitioner and Arbitrator, Karin is an established figure in the family law world. In addition to her highly successful practice, she also provides training for family lawyers and mediators and has lectured extensively on a variety of topics. She is co-author of the internationally best selling book 'Divorcing a narcissist – the lure, the loss and the law' and also 'Narcissism and Family Law – a Practitioner's Guide'.

Do It Out of Court

A Practical Guide to Alternative Dispute Resolution Processes in Family Law

Do It Out of Court

A Practical Guide to Alternative Dispute Resolution Processes in Family Law

Karin Walker

KGW Family Law

Family Lawyer, Mediator, Collaborative Practitioner and Arbitrator

Law Brief Publishing

Published 2023 by Law Brief Publishing, an imprint of Law Brief Publishing Ltd
30 The Parks
Minehead
Somerset
TA24 8BT

www.lawbriefpublishing.com

Paperback: 978-1-914608-89-6

To Grayson and Mabel

PREFACE

Since the 1990s family law practitioners have been encouraged to explore out of court dispute resolution methods to assist separating couples in resolving issues between them. Three decades later the majority of family law practitioners still have no training in specific forms of out of court practice such as mediation or collaborative law and as a consequence remain ill equipped to explain to their clients the various options which may be available to them.

In the current financial climate the funding for additional training may not be readily available. However with the court system in its current state of disarray never has it been more important for family practitioners to have the skill set to recommend alternative forms of dispute resolution other than court to their clients.

This practice guide is intended to provide a clear and practical overview of the various and extensive out of court options. It will explore with you the reasons why you as a practitioner and your practice itself will flourish notwithstanding a regular departure from the court process. It dispels the myths of the "unknown" and provides clear guidance for you to engage with your client in the option which best suits their personal circumstances.

It is hoped that you will find this guide an invaluable companion as you adapt your working methods for the future.

The law and information provided is correct as at 1st February 2023.

Karin Walker
February 2023

CONTENTS

INTRODUCTION

I hope that you are a family law practitioner with no real training in any form of out of court dispute resolution because, although also of great use to DR trained practitioners, this practice guide is specifically intended for you. It is intended to provide you with everything you need to comply with the urgent request of the President of the Family Division to keep your clients away from the Court process unless there is **ABSOLUTELY** no alternative. It is intended to dispel the myths of "suitability"; to demonstrate that almost all issues can be resolved "out of court"; to help you guide your clients to the process which is most suited to their requirements; to help you give them the best possible service. And at the same time to maintain a profitable practice.

Since lockdown the already overstretched Court service has seen applications double – in some areas even treble. The number of full time Judges has decreased. The resulting crisis is inevitable. The situation is unsustainable. The remedy lies in your hands.

It is entirely natural to lean towards the familiar. Therefore, as a consequence, we are witnessing the rise of the private FDR. Commonly seen as the most successful element of the financial remedy proceedings process – the FDR can easily be replicated. The process is identical to the court hearing of the same name – the only differences being date and venue of choice together with the specifically selected private Judge who will be totally dedicated to the couple. They will read the papers (as opposed to probably not even receiving papers until minutes before the allocated court hearing time); provide an indication which has been properly considered; but, most importantly, they want to promote their own reputation of being diligent and fair. What more could you want from your Judge!

But what about all the other options. More importantly, and particularly if the couple have children, what about helping them to develop the tools to make their own decisions, create their own outcome? Without doubt there will be times in the future when they reach another crossroads with issues to resolve. Do they always need to resort to a quasi-judicial process? Or can they look at the other alternatives which you have already helped them to consider? The private FDR is of course an excellent resource – but it is not the only one.

By the end of this guide, I hope to have sparked your interest in and enthusiasm for all forms of out of court dispute resolution. I hope that you will have opened your mind completely to what you can offer to your clients – without the need for expensive training for yourself – thereby becoming an exceptional family practitioner, ready to embrace the enormous and inevitable changes to family law practice which lie ahead. Not only able to react nimbly to them but to forge and mould the future.

SECTION ONE

FIRST CONSIDERATIONS

CHAPTER ONE

WHY, WHAT AND WHEN? THE IMPACT OF THE NEW DIVORCE LEGISLATION

6th April 2022 saw the implementation of the biggest change to divorce process in the practicing lives of us all. After decades of campaigning, "no fault" divorce finally became a reality. Either party, or the couple jointly, can issue an application for divorce with no "grounds" being cited. There follows the statutory 20-week period before application for "Conditional Order" (formerly Decree Nisi), after pronouncement of which the Court has jurisdiction to regulate financial matters by agreement or adjudication. Final Order – applied for at least six weeks and one day after the Condition Order date – brings the marriage to an end (formerly Decree Absolute).

The new process lends itself to being used by the couple alone, without recourse to the legal profession. The application is made online, the forms are relatively straightforward. The cost has reduced to just the Court fee as legal fees alongside are not really required.

The stark reality of this new process is that separating couples have no need to make a family law professional their first "port of call" when their relationship is floundering/over. The gatekeeping has radically changed. Never has it been more important for separating couples to have access to information about how to best deal with issues which will almost certainly arise. Perhaps frighteningly, an element of divorce applicants believe that the new law means they have no right to deal with financial or child arrangements except between themselves – with potentially disastrous outcomes, including no resolution or termination of financial rights and obligations.

Another concern is the impact upon the recipient of a divorce application without warning, who had no real conception of their marriage being in difficulty. Perhaps they thought they were just experiencing the "ups and downs" of married life without any grasp of the fact that their life was about to come crashing down around them.

As family law professionals, we need to create a "new normal" – making it clear that the online divorce process – now streamlined and simple – is entirely separate to resolving financial or child related issues. We need to show that those other issues can be resolved via a number of methods and that family law professionals are available to guide separating couples through the options available; to help them select the option(s) which best meets their needs and circumstances.

Of course, there will remain those individuals who need the protection of a Court ordered remedy with appropriate enforcement. Those clients need to know that family law professionals are available to help and guide them too. If those who do not need to be in the Court arena are removed from it, the Court service will be far better placed to provide those vulnerable individuals with the instant access to justice which they so desperately require.

Notwithstanding "no fault" divorce, the majority of separations will have the capacity to be fraught with emotion, to be acrimonious, to be driven by conflict and dissatisfaction. The public perception of "Court" remains that it is a place from which to obtain "justice" and "retribution". Of course, we know that neither is true. Yet our clients who find their way to us in their quest for the "clout" of the Court, have preconceived ideas of what they want and what they need. These people doubtless fall into the category described by many non-DR trained family law practitioners as "unsuitable" for anything other than an application to Court.

Those without the resources for legal advice, but with the same mindset, form the ever-growing number of litigants in person who now fill the Court lists and appear in front of the judiciary unprepared and with limited understanding of the process they have activated – thereby placing even greater pressure upon a Court service already in crisis.

Part of your role in this new "no fault" world is to create new practices so that through use, word of mouth, existing clients and social media, a message dispelling the expectation of Court and providing alternative options becomes the recognised landscape of separation for the future. It will not happen overnight. Any change which is so fundamental must be gradual and clear. You can be a fundamental part of that change.

Why is this so important? Separating couples need affordable access to information about their rights and obligations when a relationship comes to an end. Information about how to achieve an outcome which meets the needs of their family, and which is reasonable for them both. The rules governing financial outcomes are at best vague and discretionary, or at worst, incomprehensible. How do separating couples ensure that they understand what their claims are and how they can be appropriately met? In a world where their marriage can be ended with ease online, what is going to draw them to getting proper advice and information?

What information needs to be available? The MIAMS (Mediation Information and Assessment Meeting) – now expected to be more than an hour in duration – may be the best and most cost-effective way to provide the range of information required. Those meetings are conducted by accredited mediators. Might they have an inevitable leaning towards the mediation process within which they personally work – even if they additionally wear other "hats" such as "family lawyer"? Might a more streamline service be a meeting first with someone able to provide the separating person with "advice" as opposed to "information" so that they are ready to consider options with the support of someone they see as being on their side – yet still committed to finding the right out of Court method – reducing inevitable feelings of acrimony and disappointment – avoiding the idea that Court is "normal" or will be their route to "justice"?

And **When** do they need that information? Ideally at as early a stage as possible – before misconception is already causing problems – before unrealistic or unreasonable positions are maintained which become difficult to retract from.

A combination of advice aligned with neutral information is probably the ideal. The key is to marketing this service. As the family practitioner your role is vital. You might be:-

i. Advising on disclosure/valuations.

ii. Negotiating a settlement.

iii. Setting up neutral evaluation.

iv. Supporting/attending (hybrid) mediation.

v. Setting up and supporting pFDR Arbitration.

Remember also that Arbitration can be an excellent dispute resolution method for couples with limited resources. We know that those who have insufficient to meet the needs of both find division extremely difficult. These are exactly the cases which become cost disproportionate but could be resolved by the right arbitrator – even perhaps with the couple being litigants in person. Once disclosure has been provided the issue is simply how should the limited resources be divided as fairly as possible.

Think about how you can best communicate the service which you seek to offer in a manner which is clear and comprehensible. You need to demonstrate the value which a consultation with you will add – and what the initial cost is likely to be. The public are bombarded with confusing options. There is a natural scepticism of the legal profession – commonly seen as hoping to take a significant share of the separating couples' limited resources without the value or benefit being clearly outlined or indeed comprehensible. This needs to change. You can be part of that change – making you relevant and affordable. The establishment of that role will promote recommendations. As people take up your service and clearly understand the benefit, those recommendations will snowball – and also attract the vast number of separating couples who currently do not seek legal advice at all.

I sense you feeling concerned that this work does not have the "fee price tag" which you might ordinarily attract. Your long- term objective is to have a greater number of clients who will require your service for a shorter period and consequentially will have a smaller bill. But you are generating a more sustainable way of working which is therefore necessarily just as lucrative and probably more so. Makes sense? Read on.

CHAPTER TWO

THE EXPECTATION OF THE NEW CLIENT

Before you meet with any new client there are many things for you to consider and take into account:-

- How was this person referred to you?
- What (if anything) do you know about them already?
- How much courage might it have taken for them to make this appointment?
- What are the expectations of the client – and how can you best manage them?

The days of meeting with a new client with some kind of "check list" by your side are thankfully long gone. This meeting provides you with the opportunity to offer a "safe space" for your client to open up and for you to listen. A first meeting is likely to take much longer than an hour – make sure you have managed the expectations of time and cost so that everyone knows where they are. You may need to complete this first meeting at a second appointment. If this seems likely, the client will undoubtedly have recognised the value which you offer to them and see the benefit of that second meeting.

The objective of a first meeting is to let your client tell you their story. There are a number of things which you will want to find out – perhaps without expressly asking the question.

Many couples will not have a precise idea of when their relationship broke down. In almost all cases there will be a "leaver" and a "leavee". Either could be the applicant in the divorce process – or they may not yet have got that far. It will be important for you to ascertain whether your client is the decision maker in the separation process or whether they are responding to an agenda set by their partner. If the first step was not theirs, or they have reacted to an event, there may be latent hope for reconciliation of which you need to be aware as it will affect their approach.

I want to pause now and give special consideration to two particular circumstances:-

a. The "silver separators".

Although divorce is apparently on the increase, the "millennials" tend not to marry so it more is likely that your client may be in the later stages of life. Alongside all other considerations you need to factor in the impact of adult children and also the "blended" family as this may be a second (or even third) marriage. Before you understand the dynamic of the wider family members and what influence they may have over your client, in particular the self-interest of adult children, you will not have a full grasp of your client's situation. It may be very useful to create a diagram of the family tree, including all those individuals who may influence either the outcome of the breakdown of this relationship or specifically your client.

Your client, in addition to the uncertainty created by relationship breakdown, is also facing the uncertainty of everything associated with later life including retirement (or an expectation to work longer than might have been envisaged at an earlier point in their life) and also health issues alongside the inevitable stress of being perceived as the fulcrum of the family unit. You need a very particular skillset when dealing with a client at this stage in their life.

b. The victim of narcissistic abuse/the narcissist.

Initially it can be difficult to determine abuser from abusee. The closet narcissist is extremely skilled at playing the victim and is highly likely to be aligned to a successful and flamboyant partner – often easily mistaken for the exhibitionist narcissist. Or your client may not realise that they have been in an abusive relationship – only that something has felt very wrong – perhaps for many years – they may even think it has been their fault.

Whilst of course it is not your job to "self-diagnose" any form of personality disorder, an understanding of the concept and inevitable consequential issues will assist you in the provision of the best possible service for your client. In addition, narcissists thrive on the chaos and drama provided by the court process and if you are to keep this case out of court you must be aware of this and stay at least two steps ahead on behalf of the traumatised party.

Separation is completely aligned with "grief". Persistent traumatic grief can cause us to cycle (sometimes quickly) through the stages of this emotion. Those stages are:-

- Shock
- Denial
- Anger
- Bargaining
- Depression

- Acceptance
- Processing

Where is your client in their journey through the stages of grief? Do you need to wait until they reach a different stage before taking any action? To what extent might they benefit from a divorce coach? Who are the "team" of professionals with whom you work? What sort of professional relationship do you have with them? Is a team approach helpful? Who might be part of that team? Is there a need for improved financial understanding? Might specific therapy help your client get to the best possible place for making lifetime decisions? Is returning to work likely – perhaps after a significant break? The support of a return-to-work coach could be invaluable to identify what your client might be able to do – or dismiss inaccurate assertions from their partner.

Forming "a group" can feel scary – and potentially expensive but using the right professional for each specific purpose can achieve significant time and cost saving, at the same time as providing invaluable confidence boosting and empowerment.

You need to establish:-

- What does your client want?
- What do they need? (These may not be the same!)
- What are they scared of?

You are at the start of the creation of a roadmap, identifying who will be part of your journey and for how long. Get this right at the outset and you are constructing a firm base on which to set your client's springboard which will take them to a new future. See yourself as an alchemist in pursuit of a reputation for being able to create something valuable out of pain, fear, and desolation – or a simple desire to move on.

A clearer understanding of your client's need will enable you to provide a more accurate cost quote in the initial stages of the process. All too often unrealistically low cost quotes are provided at the outset of an instruction when there is optimism that matters may be resolved quickly and smoothly – plus a desire on the part of the lawyer not to lose the client through scary numbers regarding costs – which may not be accurate – and of course, a cost quote can be updated at any stage along the way. But for the client, who most certainly does not have a fund designated for "divorce costs" (or if they do, you may want to ask yourself why!!), it is much better to look at a worst-case scenario and consider how costs might then be reduced or minimised. What you do not want to create for your client is a feeling of being sucked into a process which becomes increasingly more expensive than envisaged and has the impression of being a merry-go-round from which it becomes impossible to step away.

Out of Court dispute resolution processes are far easier to cost quote because they are more capable of being contained or viewed in sections. If you always include the option of Arbitration as a final resort, you have the complete package. As costs orders are rarely made except where one party fails to meet their obligations (and even then, there is no guarantee), legal and other associated costs on divorce are "dead money" and therefore, can be factored into the negotiation process, sometimes providing a very valuable settlement tool.

Finally, be very aware that what you offer your new client following this initial consultation may be neither what they want nor what they expect. You need the skill to manage that expectation. Most people who are separating believe it is "the Court" which will be their salvation. They have an unrealistic expectation of speed and, also, of cost. After listening to and evaluating their story, you need to dispel those unrealistic expectations and present options with clarity, demonstrating value and outcome. It is those techniques which this practice guide sets out to provide.

CHAPTER THREE

YOUR PRESSURES AS A PRACTITIONER

Let's just take a moment to think about you. After all you are an individual with your own pressures, objectives, considerations, and goals.

First of all, what sort of reputation do you want to create? If it is correct that most people faced with a need to find legal advice on separation believe (albeit wrongly) that "court" is the place to go, then surely, they will be looking for someone who is apparently a champion in the court arena? Someone who is described as "the person to have in your corner", "the iron fist in a velvet glove", "a formidable adversary".

But pause to think about where most of your referrals come from. Previous (satisfied) clients. Other family law professionals. Other professional contacts. Most people are looking for a fair, reasonably rapid and not too expensive outcome. You know that the court process is the least likely to provide two and three in that list. And of course, what is "fair"? If the cost of achieving "fairness" has become disproportionate, can the outcome still be considered to be "fair"? I will leave you to think about that.

You probably have time and cost targets set which you are expected to meet. You may believe that the best way to meet those targets is through the time consuming, often repetitive, sometimes unnecessary work occasioned by the Court system where delay means repeated updating of information – avoidable within a more time efficient option for resolution. Young lawyers regularly see the number of First Appointments in their diary as a guide to being able to meet targets.

The issue of the wellbeing of family lawyers is a whole different topic – but probably my generation is responsible for this apparently overwhelming obligation. In the 1980s the family team was usually an adjunct to the litigation department – seen as a "poor relation" to the CoCo and Commercial Property teams whose transactional fees made an enormous contribution to firm profits. In any organisation "profit" is the bottom line. Money talks. The high fee earners hold position and authority.

Then came the recession of the 90s. Mortgage repossession was rife. Corporate work contracted. Family law proved to be recession proof – plus financial difficulties fuel relationship breakdown in any event. Family departments became "standalone". Niche family law firms emerged. Family law partners, for the first time, could challenge their corporate colleagues on fee income. When corporate work picked up the family law partners fought to maintain their status – only achievable on an "hourly rate" basis by teams of young lawyers churning through court-based work. Over cynical? Sadly, I don't think so. In addition, a reluctance to spend money training young lawyers in areas of out of court practice such as mediation and collaborative law began to compound the problem. Somewhat bizarrely, there is the preference in existence that you should not train in out of court dispute resolution practices until you have some significant practical experience. Whilst the benefits of maturity and experience are understood, why is it ok to represent a client in court as a trainee yet you have to wait before dipping your toe into the mediation arena for example? At the very least a 'hands on' observed understanding of what is involved at as early a stage in your career as possible must be desirable?

It then follows that as long as you are putting in the hours, you can be supporting a client in mediation or Arbitration or working collaboratively and still meeting those fee targets but through work which is more rewarding for you and more cost and time effective for your client. And probably less stressful for both of you. So you meet your targets and achieve a reputation as someone who adds value, who achieves a fairly constructed outcome in a time and cost-efficient way. Perhaps the missing link is ensuring that the public understand that this is the service they should be looking for. But only by providing that service can the link be forged. And you are focussing on your own wellbeing as well as that of your client.

CHAPTER FOUR

RAISING THE ISSUE OF OUT OF COURT DISPUTE RESOLUTION WITH YOUR CLIENT

Once you have persuaded yourself that you can maintain a profitable and relevant family law practice by first considering and engaging in out of court dispute resolution methods, you will be ready to sell the benefits of this approach to your client. As part of any first consultation your objective will be to remove any misapprehension from the mind of your client that the court process needs to be activated to achieve "justice".

As we considered in chapter 2, the client is likely to have this expectation. Their own parents may well have separated when family law fell under the banner of "litigation"; when an adversarial approach was the norm.

Don't be afraid to spell out just how inefficient the court process has become. Make it clear that although the system is there as a last resort if all else fails, your objective will be to help them achieve a satisfactory outcome without the need to place their life on hold for many months, even years; without them being subjected to:-

- Lengthy delays
- Paperwork not reaching the Judge ahead of a hearing.
- Hearings being cancelled with less than 24 hours' notice due to lack of judicial availability.

- The risk of wasted brief fees.

- A decision being made by someone who is working under unacceptable time pressure with a volume of work which is sometimes completely unmanageable.

The court system can only become "adequate", the description given to the engine of a Rolls-Royce, if some of the overloading is removed.

At this stage, don't try to explain to your client, the range of out of court options available. Remember to think about where they are on the grief cycle. There will only be so much information which they are able to take on board and retain. At this stage, they are not making decisions about process; they just need to know that there are alternatives available, and that part of your role is to find the process most likely to meet the needs of both your client and their partner. They need to go away from this meeting dissuaded that "court" is the answer – although available if absolutely required.

From your point of view, you will have listened to their story; have some idea of what sort of person they are; what their fears are; what their objectives are. You will be thinking about how best to progress matters on their behalf.

As part of this guide, you are going to look in detail at each of the out of court options in turn; examine the benefits; explore the pitfalls – all intended to help you guide your client towards making choices which are in their best interests. I said at the outset that this guide is particularly aimed at family law professionals who are not trained in any method of out of court dispute resolution process and who, consequently, do not feel confident that they fully understand the various nuances of all the various options available. In addition, you may not feel comfortable working within any one of these processes alongside your client, as your experience in this regard is limited. You don't want to lose the client. You can see the lure from this practitioner's perspective of the court process which is so very familiar. You can see just how easy it is to adopt the straightforward route. After all, your client has an initial expectation of court involvement. That is the system which you are used to. Any delay or inefficiency within that system is not your fault and you will not feel uncertain or out of your depth. This is exactly the mould which needs to be broken. The desire on the part of the practitioner to fall back to that which is familiar needs to lose its attraction.

CHAPTER FIVE

HOW TO APPROACH THE "OTHER SIDE"

So far as we have been focussing on your client – meeting their needs and managing their expectations. But there are of course two people involved in any separation. Out of court dispute resolution remains voluntary. How many times have you heard the claim – "well I would recommend out of court methods but the "other side" refuse to agree/are running the case for their client in a way which makes out of court dispute resolution impossible/refuse to engage at all." In reality, how many times have you been that "other side"?

The two main arguments employed by family law practitioners against the use of out of court dispute resolution are:-

- My client thinks it is unsuitable.
- The "other side" won't agree.

The truth is that almost every case is suitable and if family practitioners take the approach proposed by this guide the intransigence of the "other side" must necessarily fall away.

In any case, making an early approach to the "other side" is important. If a solicitor or family law professional is already instructed the most positive course of action is to pick up the phone to them. Increasingly we live in a world where interaction is handled remotely, more often than not via the sterility of electronic communication. There is no substitute for speaking to someone. You may know them already. If you do not, you want to get to know them and seek to build a rapport at the earliest stage possible. It is very hard to audibly state that you are not interested in entering into a constructive dialogue and are not prepared to consider options. You might try to hide behind "my client sees it as unsuitable for their situation" but such contention can be readily and plausibly challenged.

If the "other side" is currently unrepresented, your initial approach will more likely be in writing, so it is not open to misinterpretation. You might say something along these lines: -

> *Dear Chris,*
>
> *I have been consulted by your (spouse) Alex as a consequence of their perception that your relationship has broken down. Alex has reached the conclusion that steps need to be taken to formalise your separation. This is a difficult time for you both and for your family. You will both need to make important decisions about your future. Ideally, you will need to construct an outcome together with the assistance of professional advice and support.*
>
> *I do recommend that you seek advice from a family law professional. If you do not have details of any such person to hand, I would refer you to the website of Resolution at www.resolution.org where you will find details of specialist family lawyers listed by geographical location.*
>
> *I look forward to working with you and your representative alongside Alex to resolve matters in a manner which is in the best interests of you both (and your children).*
>
> *I look forward to hearing from either you or your representative as soon as possible so that we can discuss matters further.*
>
> *Yours etc.*

Your aim is to create an environment which will promote constructive discussion – not cause positional polarisation. You are dealing with a couple who were once in love; who may have brought up a family together. Feelings may have changed; trust may have been lost but there will be some basis still there which you can build upon. You are looking for the commonality which may still exist. Probably both parties want a fair and time efficient outcome. They don't want to spend a prolonged period in limbo. Probably neither wants this to cost a fortune. Hopefully both want what is best for their children. These are all good places to start.

Of course, if one of the couple suffers from narcissistic personality disorder (or similar) you may have an uphill struggle on your hands. But if you understand the disorder and how to help your client stay two steps ahead of the manipulation and abuse, you might still be able to avoid court.

This first communication is so very important and needs to be done quickly before "battle lines" are inadvertently set. Get it right and you have taken an enormous first step in the right direction. And you may find that the "other side" is not as belligerent as you anticipated but in fact on the same page as you.

Once the "other side" has taken advice, pick up the phone to their lawyer. Start to make a plan.

CHAPTER SIX

THE REAL PURPOSE OF THE MIAM AND HOW TO GET THE BEST OUT OF THAT APPOINTMENT

How do you regard the MIAM (Mediation Information and Assessment Meeting)? Is it a slightly tedious and arguably unnecessary step which needs to be taken to issue a Form A or C100? Or is it really an inexpensive way of obtaining clear information from a person accredited to provide such information about all forms of out of court dispute resolution and their respective merits and benefits.

If you feel that you do not have a clear understanding of all of the options because you are unfamiliar with them, send your client to someone who is trained to provide the necessary information with clarity and enthusiasm. If mediation might ultimately be an option, go to the person who would likely be the mediator (or one of a list) of your choice. If you think hybrid mediation, with the ability on the part of the mediator to hold confidences, is the desired way forwards, make sure you select a hybrid trained mediator.

Build a rapport with a group of such professionals so that you build a professional relationship. This will result in cross-referrals derived from mutual respect.

The person conducting the MIAM will write to the other party inviting them to attend a similar meeting. If you already have a dialogue with their representative, they are hopefully providing the same steer as you. If their client won't attend a MIAM you can ask them why not.

If your fear is that the "other side" will not engage and that you need to issue a court application simply to set time frame parameters and demonstrate that your client "means business", a Form FM1 can be signed within four months of the MIAM appointment at no additional cost. This issue of a court application does not rule out 'out of court' dispute resolution – far from it. Whilst it may set a mark in the sand, it will hopefully bring the other person to the out of court negotiating table – aware that things really do need to be resolved.

You may wish to consider attending the MIAM meeting with your client. It could be of benefit for you to be on hand to discuss the possible out of court options with the mediator. You may wish to encourage the other side's representative to do so also. Remember that the MIAM is a pre-meeting to the process of mediation or other form of dispute resolution process. The purpose is to consider what might be the best method of dispute resolution process to suit the particular needs of this couple.

CHAPTER SEVEN

THE BESPOKE NATURE OF THE OUT OF COURT METHODS OF DISPUTE RESOLUTION

Perhaps the greatest fear which practitioners have of the out of court resolution methods is feeling out of their depth; a nervousness that this is a process with which they are not entirely familiar. The court system informs a structure which has been in place for many years. With its recognised pattern, coupled with the process being embedded within a national institution – the Family Justice System – a name which perpetuates the suggestion of "fairness" and "justice" – there is a sense of feeling "safe". That can be just as important for a practitioner as it is for their client.

What we know as family law professionals, however, is that every case is different. Although this discretionary jurisdiction makes it almost impossible to accurately predict an outcome with certainty, it is exactly this which makes our role so interesting, varied and rewarding and which ensures that our clients and their families are treated as individuals with their individual circumstances having relevance. Add that concept to the very bespoke nature of all forms of out of court process and you create a system which will operate under guidelines but in a way which maintains and supports the individuality of every family.

So, to recap on your approach: -

- Spend time finding out about your client at the outset – what sort of person are they? Where are they on their separation journey? What are their fears? What are their aspirations?

- Dispel misunderstandings about pursuing "justice", "fairness" or "retribution" at an early stage. Make it clear that the court is not the place to achieve any of this. Manage the expectations of your client. Encourage them to recognise that the needs and entitlements of both parties to the relationship must be considered in tandem within the confines of the resources available to them.

- Establish a dialogue with the "other side" as soon as possible. Encourage joint decisions about process, staying future and family focused. Think about how this couple will co-parent their children long after the involvement of lawyers is no longer required.

- There is no magic in the court being able to ensure that full and frank disclosure is provided. A direct explanation, especially from a jointly instructed facilitator, can often be far more powerful than any order made by a court. The court is, however, always available if belligerence sets in on either side – with undoubted cost consequences.

- Woking within a process where you have almost complete control will be far more empowering for the couple – and also for you as a participating advisor.

- Think about the reputation which you intend to build and why. How does that best enable you to maintain your obligations to your firm? How does it enable you, more importantly, to maintain your obligations to yourself?

SECTION TWO

THE OUT OF COURT OPTIONS AND HOW THEY WORK IN PRACTICE

Even now, the "out of court" options for dispute resolution are seen as "alternative". The word "alternative" in this context means "different to that which is in existence". The suggestion therefore is that there is a "normal" way of doing things, but you might choose an "alternative".

Perhaps, what we as family law practitioners need to strive towards is a situation where out of court options become normal practice. The court option would then be activated only in circumstances where there is simply no choice. Increasingly, we are seeing members of the Family Law Bar metaphorically tying up the pink ribbon on their adversarial practice and moving towards a career in mediation, arbitration, or private FDR work – or a mixture of all three. Some may perceive this as such individuals not having "cut it" completely at the Bar but, in fact, these undisputedly frontrunners are stealing a march in what is now a fast-changing landscape. In addition, there is absolutely no reason why junior members of the Family Law Bar (or more junior family law professionals) should not seek to establish a practice in straightforward small money cases where agreement simply cannot be achieved but where a neutral evaluation or pFDR might assist. It is worth bearing in mind that neither require any specific formal qualification.

I am going to take you through each form of out of court method of working – looking at the benefits but, perhaps more importantly, also the potential pitfalls. Uncertainty and a fear of the unknown has to date caused practitioners not trained in these areas themselves to shy away – perhaps also concerned about the loss of a client or even insurance issues if they are asked to deal with the preparation of an order which emerges from a negotiation in which they have had little direct involvement.

So, let's look, in detail, at the alternatives.

CHAPTER EIGHT

MEDIATION AND HYBRID MEDIATION

The practice of mediation dates to Ancient Greece. Many ancient philosophers have recognised the importance of mediation. By way of example, Confucius adhered to the "no litigation" concept, acknowledging that all disputes could be resolved through harmony and cooperation.

Mediation came to the fore in the UK in the area of family law in the 1990s and is possibly the best form of dispute resolution not involving court from the point of view of the public – largely due to the need to attend a "Mediation Information and Assessment Meeting" in advance of the issue of any form of court application, save in the most exceptional of cases.

Let's look first at what have been the historic problems regarding mediation and why practitioners have rejected this as an option.

1. Losing the client to another process.
2. Lack of confidence in the mediator.
3. Fear that any agreement reached may not be in the best interests of the client.
4. Concerns about not being involved in the negotiation process.
5. Potentially having to "start all over again" if it doesn't work.

Although mediation is more clearly in the public domain than other methods of dispute resolution, the process is still not readily or fully understood. A courtroom drama remains far more "exciting" from a media perspective. On the rare occasion that characters in the mainstream soaps such as *Coronation Street* or *Eastenders* have engaged in the process, it has appeared somewhat unprofessional and unsuccessful. It doesn't justify the same level of "sensation" as a day in court.

So, what are some of the main elements of the process? First let's look at the area of financial remedy.

1. The Neutral Facilitator

   The mediator is someone in whom both of the couple can place their trust to guide and inform them along their journey to reach an outcome which both can live with and, more importantly, understand why the outcome on which they have alighted is fair to them both. The role of the mediator is to listen to each of the couple, to provide a safe space where they can address the issues which are important to each of them and say things to one another which may need to be expressed for progress to be made. The mediator will use their skills to:

   - Address any power imbalance between the couple to ensure a neutral and level playing field.

   - Ensure that full and frank disclosure is provided and explain the problems which will arise if either of the couple fail to comply with their obligations in this respect. The exercise to be undertaken is "what is there and how should it be divided?" Without properly completing stage one it is impossible to move to stage two. There is nothing about a court order which will ensure the production of full disclosure. Often it is far more powerful for someone neutral working alongside the couple to explain why disclosure is an obligation which needs to be complied with.

- "Reality test" suggested proposals.

- Put forward possible options which might be worth considering based on the mediator's experience.

- Form a working relationship with the couple based upon trust and professional boundaries and support.

2. A Safe Space

Mediation is a "without prejudice" or "privileged" process. This means that the couple can put forward ideas and consider options safe in the knowledge that if they prove to be unworkable, they will be put to one side rather than be brought back to "haunt them" in any way. The couple cannot reach a binding agreement in mediation – they can only alight on a set of proposals with which they are prepared to move forwards. Proposals will only become a binding agreement once the couple have had the opportunity to take legal advice if they wish to do so. The mediator will prepare a Memorandum of Understanding which will set out in clear terms the issues discussed and the proposals under consideration.

3. The Role of the Lawyers

We have already looked at the lawyer's fear that they may lose their client to the process and then be expected to draft an order, the basis of which they do not properly understand. It is a common misapprehension that it is the hybrid mediation process which involves lawyers in the mediation. This is in fact incorrect. The nature of hybrid mediation will be dealt with separately. Lawyers can be fully involved in mediation at any time. In fact, mediation is sometimes described as "a game for five players" – the mediator, the couple and their respective lawyers. The mediation process itself will be managed by the mediator on behalf of the couple – it is important to remember that the explicit role of the lawyers will be as follows: -

- To provide initial advice for their client.
- To deal with disclosure and provide the mediator with either an agreed asset schedule or a schedule showing any areas of disagreement to be discussed and resolved in the mediation.
- To support their client either within the process or alongside.
- To advise on the proposed outcome prior to it becoming a binding agreement.
- To draft the paperwork to achieve a court order by consent.

Incorrectly, it has often been assumed that mediation only works for couples who are by and large "on the same page". Mediation can achieve successful resolution for the most acrimonious of couples. The couple (or one of them) may want to stay separate at all times. This can be facilitated with separate break out rooms either remotely or in person. Either or both of the couple may want to have their lawyer with them during the process. This can be extremely beneficial – especially if the couple are to remain in separate breakout rooms. Sometimes there is a nervousness that this will make the process very expensive. Although the day of the meeting may feel expensive with the fees for one's own lawyer plus 50% of the mediator's fee being incurred, in reality, you are just concentrating the cost and actually can make significant savings. The presence of the lawyers at the mediation session means that each of the couple can take instant advice as options are considered, as opposed to doing so in between sessions. The benefits of this are:

- Delay between sessions while advice is taken on both sides which can cause the negotiation thread to unravel is avoided.

- The mediation sessions remain focussed and potentially fast moving due to the instant access to advice.

- The mediator is aware of the advice which each of the couple is receiving during the process.

- If acceptable proposals are identified there is no need for the mediator to draft a Memorandum of Understanding as both lawyers know exactly what is under consideration – a clear cost saving for the couple.

- If everyone is content that the proposals should become a binding agreement, the process can step out of the veil of privilege and become open, so that the open agreement can be confirmed – deal done! If it is achievable, the lawyers might even draft the consent order there and then. At the very least the couple could – if everyone feels comfortable – leave the process with signed Heads of Terms.

The involvement of lawyers in the mediation process can be a central part of the process known as **The Certainty Project** – combining mediation with arbitration. This will be outlined in detail below and in chapter 13.

As already indicated, hybrid mediation is distinguished from what might be called "classic" mediation only by the fact that the mediator can hold confidences. This will be covered in greater detail below.

4. Arbitration

The Certainty Project emerged from the notion that what separating couples want is either to be helped to resolve their own dispute or to have somebody make a decision for them. Whilst the success rate of mediation is high, inevitably, there may be those issues which cannot simply be resolved through discussion. Were the mediation process to break down and the couple refer matters to the Family Court, the principal difficulties would be as follows: -

- The delay of about 12 to 18 months before resolution could be achieved.
- Significant resulting cost because of such delay.
- The inability of the court to adopt a “nimble” approach.

An arbitrator can, either on paper or via oral hearing, decide all issues in a case or simply those issues which remain outstanding. If there is only one outstanding issue, the arbitrator may be able to resolve that extremely quickly and cost-effectively via an “on paper” exercise. Joint instructions for the arbitration can be provided by the mediator. This is particularly relevant where the couple may not have solicitors involved. Their financial position may be such that their resources are extremely limited. It is often the “small money” cases which are the most difficult to resolve as, in circumstances where there is insufficient to meet the needs of both, giving ground can be difficult. Compromise can be extremely hard to achieve. The mediator can send the couple into arbitration. The couple may each (or either one) wish to take advice on specific tasks such as perhaps the preparation of a section 25 statement. The beauty of this bespoke service is that it can be specifically tailored to suit the needs and budget of each individual couple.

5. An Ongoing Point of Contact

   It is becoming increasingly common to prescribe that should further issues arise between the couple at any stage in the future they will, in the first instance, engage in the process of mediation to resolve such issues. Building a relationship with a mediator and the process itself creates a comfortable feeling of familiarity within which this can be achieved.

So how might all of this apply to child related issues?

When you are dealing with child arrangements perhaps one of the most important benefits of the mediation process is the opportunity to create a forum to which the couple can readily return very quickly in the event that future issues arise. They can enlist the help of an (already trusted) neutral facilitator before positions are taken, the fallout from which could adversely impact on the child/ren.

"The voice of the child" is an enormously valuable tool. It does not need to be confined to issues relating to the child/ren themselves but can even be employed to hear the impact of ongoing disputes in financial matters upon the children where appropriate. Remember all out of court options are completely bespoke – pick the tools which will suit and assist each individual couple.

The children will be brought into the process with the agreement of both parents. Pause to consider whether you would want to use the same mediator to see the child/ren or bring in someone else. If your initial mediator is not qualified to see the child/ren the decision is made for you but when might you otherwise bring in someone else?

Any meeting with the child/ren is confidential to them – the parents will only be told what the child/ren agree should be divulged (save of course for safeguarding issues). The mediator will write to the child/ren in an age-appropriate way to offer them the opportunity to attend a meeting. Whether or not they do so is their choice. They will be reassured that their parents will not discuss the meeting with them either beforehand or afterwards. The mediator will impress upon the parents the importance of this.

The views obtained from the child/ren are not admissible in the Court context – this forms part of the "without prejudice" element of the mediation process.

It is preferable for the children to be taken to a meeting by another relative or family friend rather than either of the parents, so there can be no suggestion of any influence. The mediator will then arrange a feedback session with Mum and Dad.

This can be a very powerful tool as most parents are keen to do the best for their child/ren. What is often revealed is that the child/ren have been trying to make things better between their parents in a very naive way, often making things worse and telling each parent what they think they may want to hear. The classic example of this is saying that Mum/Dad's new partner is unkind and even nasty to them because they are scared to admit they get on with them okay. Also what is important to the child/ren is often quite different to the issues raised by the parents.

It is important to remember that child arrangements have nothing to do with arithmetic. Parental responsibility lies 100% with both parents. Most mediations involving child arrangements have little to do with the child/ren and everything to do with "unfinished business" between the parents. Always think about whether a family consultant or divorce coach would help this family. If you suggest this make sure that you normalise it – no one likes to think they need help.

Mediation is an excellent forum for the construction of a child arrangements plan. When you are contemplating the issue of a Form C100 think about what it is your client wants to achieve. Of course, if an urgent prohibitive steps order is needed you may have no choice other than to issue. Similarly, if one parent is refusing to allow the child/ren to see the other, and refuses to engage in a dialogue, you may have no choice but if you are trying to agree child arrangements what actual benefit is a court order? The needs of the child/ren will change. If one parent refuses to adhere to an imposed outcome, what are you going to do about it? Shortly it is better that the parents work together with help from supportive professionals to construct an outcome – and what a great message that sends to the child/ren. Even if you feel you must issue an application in relation to an issue which appears entirely binary you should still work at creating a discursive environment prior to any hearing – it can only be better for the family. It is a rare parent who does not ultimately put the interests of the child/ren above their own. If they are clearly incapable of doing so, you may be dealing with someone who has a personality disorder meaning that they just can't care about anyone (not even the children) in place of themselves – useful to have an indication of this at an early stage.

The Children Act 1989 says that there should be no order unless parents are unable to agree. Therefore, you would simply record any child arrangements agreement openly. If, however either parent does not comply – whilst the best next step may be to return to mediation to find out why – you could always turn that agreement into an order via a court application for enforcement purposes if you felt that you really had to.

It is easy to think that lawyer support is less necessary when child arrangements are under discussion, but lawyer support can be invaluable to keep that discussion on track – and of course the meeting can move from "without prejudice" to "open" allowing proposed terms to become an immediately binding agreement.

Hybrid Mediation

We have touched on the fact that the only difference between "classic" and "hybrid" mediation is the ability on the part of the mediator to hold confidences. Remember the refrain – "oh yes, mediation is great – but just not suitable in this case". Hybrid mediation is potentially suitable for almost every case. It can be used, in particular, for those couples in high conflict, perhaps even where there has been some form of abuse or violence. After all is court really the right place for someone who has lived through such an emotional trauma? Surely it is better to be able to remain in separate breakout rooms, be supported by your lawyer and (the difference) be able to tell the mediator how you feel, what scares you, what is important to you, what has happened to you, all in complete confidence.

Most mediators who have trained in the hybrid model only work in this way thereafter because the option to hold confidences beyond the intake session can be extremely helpful. These mediators are specifically trained to manage high conflict situations for people who after all still need to find some form of resolution and often in high conflict situations speed (which is very difficult to achieve in the court system) is vital.

It is a common misconception that "hybrid" mediation is the model which involves lawyers. This is completely incorrect. Lawyers can be involved to such greater or lesser extent as suits the individual couple in any form of mediation. The presence of lawyers within the mediation process can be hugely beneficial. From the point of view of the lawyer, the concern about passing a client into the mediation process who only returns with a Memorandum of Understanding (which, at first glance, can be difficult to follow due to a lack of involvement in the process ongoing) inevitably causes apprehension. If you are not planning on attending the mediation process at all as a supporting solicitor, at the very least you may ask the mediator to copy you into any notes arising from each session, so that you remain abreast of the negotiation (of course, with the agreement and instruction of your client).

The attendance of lawyers at the sessions themselves can be seen as an additional and unnecessary overlay of cost. It can make the day of the mediation session feel very expensive. But let's just drill down into what happens. Mediation is a without prejudice process and agreements cannot be achieved without the couple taking independent legal advice. If that legal advice is with him "in the room" it means that the negotiation process becomes much more focused and the pace increases. Rather than accumulating issues over which advice is required, the advice can be provided instantly, thereby allowing the mediated discussion to progress to the next stage. Although of course there is a cost for the attendance of the lawyer, this is simply a cost which would be incurred at a later stage. Further, the requirements for both parties to take independent advice separately and outside of the mediation process will give rise to a "lull" in the process whilst this takes place, sometime for several weeks. Momentum can be lost. Progress can be unravelled.

If the couple alight upon a set of proposals with which they are content to move forwards and have their lawyers with them in the mediation, that mediation can be converted into an "open" meeting at which a binding agreement can be achieved. At the very least, Heads of Terms can be drafted and signed. In some cases, it may even be possible to prepare the draft order by consent.

A further cost saving is that the mediator will have no requirement to prepare a Memorandum of Understanding. Both lawyers have a full understanding of the mediation which has just taken place and will have made their own notes. They will both feel comfortable to advise their respective clients without additional documentation being prepared – a further cost saving for the couple.

So, how actually does hybrid mediation work?

i. The first step is for each of the couple to attend an intake session with the mediator. In particular, the mediator will assess whether this is a high conflict couple. Remember that hybrid mediation is the process particularly suited to those couples who might otherwise litigate. A decision will be made as to whether the couple should remain in separate breakout rooms (either remote or in person). It is important that each of the couple feel that they are in a "safe space" to progress their negotiation.

ii. If it is intended that solicitors will support their clients in mediation (or perhaps only one will do so), a professionals meeting will be arranged. In the event that only one of the couple is represented, the unrepresented party would also attend that professionals meeting. The purpose is to "scope out" the mediation itself. It is important for any lawyers involved to recognise that this is the mediator's process and as such they oversee the mediation itself. The role of the lawyers is to provide support and advice.

iii. It may be beneficial for the lawyers to deal with exchange of financial information on a voluntary basis and to deal with any questions which might arise from the same ahead of the first mediation session. The mediator can then be provided either with an agreed asset schedule or an asset Schedule highlighting the area of dispute. This approach has the benefit of the lawyers feeling comfortable with the levels of disclosure provided and removes the need for the mediator to spend significant time (and therefore incur significant cost for the couple) reading through the disclosure documents. This is particularly relevant as the mediator will not be "advising" in relation to the same.

iv. Ahead of the first joint session, an agenda will be prepared by the mediator and circulated to all involved. By this stage, the hybrid mediation agreement will have been signed by both of the couple and any participating lawyers. Whilst the lawyers can provide input to the proposed agenda, it is for the mediator to settle this document, taking account of the issues raised by each of the couple. The mediator may wish to commence the first session with all parties together in the (virtual) room. This provides an opportunity for everyone involved to meet and, particularly, for each of the couple to recognise that the other's lawyer is simply there to try to help this family reach resolution. For those couples, however, who simply cannot have any form of contact with their partner, staggered arrival or log in times will be arranged to ensure that each is safely placed in their individual breakout room right at the outset.

v. The mediator will use their ability to hold confidences to elicit information from each of the couple which may assist their facilitation of the negotiation. They will, however, be encouraging each of the couple to give permission for that confidential information to be disclosed to the other side where appropriate. Where possible, the mediator will be looking for opportunities to bring the couple together in the same (virtual) room if they would feel comfortable with this.

vi. If acceptable proposals are reached, the mediator can consider turning the mediation into an "open" forum and hand over to the lawyers to conclude matters.

So, let's recap. Mediation works extremely well in almost all circumstances. The couple can be supported by their lawyers throughout and in fact this is probably a very good version of the process. Mediation provides a safe space for even the most high conflict couples and the mediator quickly becomes a source of neutral support and provides an environment to which future issues can be brought for resolution – particularly important for child arrangements or variations to financial support.

Of course not every client can afford to involve their lawyer in the mediation process, particularly where separate meetings are maintained for the couple and there may be periods where, when the mediator is with one of the couple, the other is simply waiting. An alternative to having your lawyer by your side throughout the session is to have them available on the telephone. You may agree with your client that you will block out the time of the mediation session so that if you are needed, you be telephoned directly. You can easily be getting on with other paperwork while you await a call. From the client's perspective they are only paying for the time involved in providing specific advice which is required.

Once again, I want to underline the very bespoke nature of all out of court dispute resolution methods. The overriding objective is to achieve an outcome which meets the needs of the couple involved. How that is achieved is something available for adaptation.

But this is only one option – let's look at others.

CHAPTER NINE

NEUTRAL EVALUATION

In my view this is one of the most beneficial yet underutilised forms of dispute resolution. Inexpensive and very quick to arrange, it is a great resource at all kinds of pivotal moments in any negotiation. Neutral evaluation can be used as a "stand alone" remedy or be brought into other forms of dispute resolution where an impasse has been reached. Obvious moments for consideration of the use of this out of court dispute resolution method are: -

1. Right at the outset of a case. You may identify at an early stage that there is an issue (or maybe even several) which could easier be argued either way. Examples of these might be:

    a. Can any resources be "ring-fenced" as being pre-acquired or for other reasons be seen as outside of the matrimonial acquest?

    b. To what extent might non-matrimonial resources be invaded because of "need"?

    c. How should an interest in a company run by one spouse be paid out if there are not the funds to pay out now? How do you rationalise only one party working in the business moving forwards (post separation endeavours) with the fact that funds belonging to the other spouse remain invested in the business?

    d. Equalisation of pension value or income in retirement?

    This list is far from exhaustive.

2. In the process of (hybrid mediation). You may have reached an impasse. Neutral evaluation brought into the process through the neutrality of the mediator can really help to keep the mediation on track and help iron out those “bumpy issues”. This applies just as much in children’s cases as it does in financial remedy, particularly where the issue(s) are quite binary, and an objective view might be helpful. How often in a mediation might one or other of the couple ask – “Well, what would you do in my situation?”. That is not a question which the mediator can answer, but it may flag up the need to bring in a neutral evaluator.

   Neither party is compelled to accept the view of the neutral evaluator, but they may be foolish not to do so.

3. In a collaborative case. When we consider collaborative practice in detail, we shall look at the range of options available to break impasse and move the negotiation forwards – of which neutral evaluation is one. Used in a very similar way to how it is used in mediation but here rather than the mediator providing neutral information the two solicitors working together will do so. The joint selection of an evaluator in whom both parties and their representatives have confidence is key to the evaluation achieving the desired effect.

   How might you select a neutral evaluator?

   There is no requirement to have any form of specific qualification to be neutral evaluator. You will want to select someone who has the skills to deal with the particular issue; has the “gravitas” to inspire confidence in the couple; and suit the budget of the case. A sensible starting point might be those who are qualified as arbitrators – but do consider more junior members of the Bar and also solicitors if the facts and the resources of the couple suggest that this might be the appropriate way forwards. Don’t rule out solicitors who may be very well placed to provide the guidance you require in a clear and cost-effective way.

Neutral evaluation is something to which you should be giving consideration in almost every case – trying to iron out the points which cause the couple to become positional and therefore logjammed and getting a view that assists the ongoing negotiation at as early a stage as possible. Of course, you might use your neutral evaluator to give an overall view about the case. In circumstances, however, where the couple would prefer not to lose ownership of the overall outcome, a single sticking point is often more likely to be the issue over which assistance is required.

If this is something you have not used before, try thinking about how useful it might be at the outset of this case. You will be surprised by the impact on the resolution of "tricky" issues.

CHAPTER TEN

COLLABORATIVE PRACTICE

When collaborative law was first brought to this jurisdiction by Pauline Tessler in or around 2002, it was seen as a revolutionary way to resolve disputes between separating couples. Family lawyers, particularly those in niche family law practices, were keen to engage in this new method which involved the two lawyers working together via a series of four-way meetings, where all advice was given openly and the group of four would work together to find an outcome which was for the overall benefit of the family. The venue for each meeting would alternate between the offices of the two participating lawyers with the host keeping the notes and also providing carefully chosen finger food intended to promote the conciliatory atmosphere.

All parties to the process would sign a document known as a "Participation Agreement". Other professionals could be joined to the process, such as a family coach or consultant, a financial advisor, the parties' accountant and of course, as referred to in chapter 9, a neutral evaluator or indeed any other professional who may be of help.

For a few years, collaborative practice was extremely buoyant. "PODS" were established in local groups to encourage the promotion of this method of working and to build groups of like-minded practitioners with the intention of cross-referring work. Other professionals, such as IFAs, would also joint the PODS. A practice community grew.

Unfortunately, this worked better in some areas than others. In most rural areas it was hard to establish a POD. The fact that both parties agreed not to issue court proceedings was seen as very beneficial – a major and explicit move towards a true "out of court" form of practice. Those who were in more rural or geographically distanced practices looked to joining a number of PODS which were relatively proximate.

The problem, however, was that if the process broke down, both of the couple would have to find new representation. Lawyers found themselves drawing this to the attention of their clients right at the outset. They were keen to ensure that their clients understood the "downside" of this process before they embarked upon it. When you have made the huge decision to take advice about bringing your relationship to an end and selected a lawyer in whom to place you trust, the last thing you want to consider is a process which might mean you have to start all over again with someone else. Remember we considered the grief cycle. A client who is still in shock or angry will not want to even contemplate such a situation. It became easy for that lawyer, who I shall call "the other side" to persuade their client that this was not a process for them.

We then saw the advent of "collaborative lite" in an attempt to avoid this situation. This meant simply not signing a participation agreement but, otherwise, the process remained the same. The absence of a participation agreement meant that if a court application had to be made, the lawyers could still remain instructed in the case. Purist collaborative practitioners felt this was "tinkering" with the process to too great an extent. This was a situation where labels got in the way of focusing on an outcome for the couple.

For these and a number of other reasons, collaborative practice slowly became less fashionable – no longer the "new kid on the block" but, rather, a process which seemed to carry too many procedural or practice difficulties. With the requirement to attend a MIAM as a prerequisite to court proceedings, mediation, again, stepped to the fore. Of course, many collaborative practitioners are also trained mediators, so it just became a "change of hat" for them. Some collaborative practitioners who had developed a thriving local practice supported by other like-minded lawyers continued to work well within this collaborative method, but it would be fair to say popularity waned.

But then with arbitration gradually being on the increase, a corner was turned. Arbitration is simply another form of out of court dispute resolution method. Why, therefore, would you need to change lawyer if you were simply unable to agree through a four-way negotiation but needed someone to make a decision for you? It was accepted that a move to arbitration would not require a change of representation. Collaborative practice saw a resurgence of popularity: another very bespoke method of dispute resolution.

So how does it work?

Both parties instruct a collaboratively trained practitioner. Each of the couple decide upon a mission statement – what is really important to them in this process. It might be as simple as "to achieve a fair outcome", or it may be more specific, e.g., "to have financial help and confidence that outgoings can be met through personal endeavours", or as blunt as "to keep the house" or "to achieve a clean break".

Negotiation does not take place in writing. A series of four-way meetings will be arranged to work through the process of "what is there and how should we divide it?". Financial information is provided on an open basis but, otherwise, all discussions are "without prejudice". Both representatives will provide their advice in front of the other party and their lawyer. Nothing can be "lost in translation". Everything is transparent. This is extremely beneficial – but if there is a difference of opinion, neutral evaluation may be the way to resolve it.

If agreement cannot be achieved, an arbitrator is best placed to make the decision over "how do we divide it". The process for that reason lends itself to the initial negotiation process within the Certainty Project model in place of (hybrid) mediation. If you feel that you do not need a decision to be made but that the process could be eased by the couple each being able to speak confidentially to a neutral facilitator, you may want to bring in a hybrid mediator to manage the negotiation.

Hopefully, you can now see the way in which all of these out of court processes can interlink; that your role as the instructed representative is to fully understand how each works, so that you can create a bespoke negotiation specifically suited to the needs and requirements of each individual case. This combination of skill and creativity will help you build the reputation you seek as a practitioner and encourage referrals, the intention being to increase your client base but reduce the amount of time you need to spend with each individual client. The result is a greater number of clients all with smaller bills. This business model ought to have the effect of encouraging into the legal process those who might otherwise have stayed away for fear of extortionate legal fees. Such individuals may have historically resolved issues badly or not at all – storing up major difficulties for the future. If cost-effective methods which add value are readily and regularly available, proper professional assistance in the event of separation becomes less daunting and more affordable. Take-up will inevitably increase.

CHAPTER ELEVEN

THE PRIVATE FDR

The private FDR (or pFDR) is the form of out of court dispute resolution which most closely follows the standard court process. Seen by many as the stage within the court process most likely to achieve settlement, it is rapidly becoming the most used form of out of court method, particularly in London. With the court system becoming riddled with delay and the consequential adverse impact on separating couples leaving them in limbo for an unreasonable and often intolerable period of time, it is becoming quite common to set up a pFDR shortly after completion of financial disclosure. So why is this the case? As the pFDR completely mirrors the court equivalent, the process is entirely familiar, Inevitably, it is favoured by the Bar for the same reasons. For a relatively modest cost, you will secure the services of a pFDR Judge who will

- read the papers.
- be exclusively available to you all day on a date and at a venue of your choice.
- will want a reputation for being fair and diligent.

The pFDR Judge will provide the couple with an indication of what they think a Judge might do if the case were to go to a final hearing. You may ask yourself what the difference between that and a neutral evaluation is. The neutral evaluation is a clear view about an outcome. The pFDR Judge is unlikely to be quite so categoric. The pFDR Judge is not deciding the case. He/she cannot impose any outcome on the couple and must strive therefore to maintain the momentum of negotiation at the same time as providing clear guidance. The difference is subtle but important.

The success rate of the pFDR is seen to be high. It can, however, also be seen as quite an expensive day out. If you sense that one of the couple plans only to go through the motion – perhaps because they suffer from narcissistic personality disorder and are just playing games to prolong the chaos and drama – it may not be the right way forwards. Make sure you know your couple. Just like neutral evaluation, there is no specific qualification required to be a pFDR Judge. You may, however, want someone who is a trained arbitrator or sits in a judicial capacity. But if your couple is of modest means don't rule out a junior solicitor or barrister who may be very suited to the case. (Also think about whether this is an area of practice which you might like to develop for yourself).

It is always a good idea to involve the couple in the choice of pFDR Judge. Let the lawyers choose a group of six with whom both are content and then let one of the couple reduce the group to three and the other make the final decision. If one of the couple does suffer from NPD it is a good idea to let them have the final choice (final word). It will make them feel in control in a situation which makes no difference, as both lawyers would be happy to select all six of the possible candidates.

CHAPTER TWELVE

ARBITRATION

Arbitration is the private adjudication process within the out of court options. It was first available in financial proceedings in 2012 and was extended to cover children's proceedings in 2016. Despite the obvious benefits over the court process: -

- Choice of Judge – who will want to be seen as both diligent and fair
- Choice of venue
- Choice of date
- A bespoke service
- Complete privacy
- Ease of communication with your Arbitrator during the process
- Swift interlocutory decisions where required.

take up has been relatively slow, particularly in children's proceedings. The likely reason for this in children's proceedings is that delay will always suit one parent. Of course, it will not suit the children who can only be adversely affected by uncertainty and the knowledge that their parents are locked in dispute over arrangements for them. (Think about the need to stress this to your client who might favour delay).

Again, arbitration has been thwarted by the "other side" taking the view that the process is "unsuitable". Mystifying, I know. How could a bespoke service that is quicker, cheaper, and better considered because proper time is available for such consideration be "unsuitable"? I would say that almost every case that could be litigated can be arbitrated.

How does arbitration work?

The first step is to agree with the other side that arbitration would be beneficial. For the reasons listed above it would be hard to see how an application to Court could be preferable.

The couple could be at various stages in their process: -

i. They may be right at the beginning of the process. Remember the section dealing with client expectation. Try to replace the idea of "court" with "arbitration" if an adjudication is required. Underline the benefits right at the start of your instruction.

ii. The couple may already be in mediation. Your client may be concerned about lack of progress or nervous about lack of disclosure. You may ask the mediator to sign a Form FM1 but notwithstanding the fact that your client is prepared to continue with the mediation but simply to set a time frame to bring matters to a conclusion and also provide the facility of a court application if some form of interim order might be required. Consideration of Form FM1 will identify that there is no "box" for the mediator to tick which deals with this eventuality. Rather than looking to issue a Form A in these circumstances, sign up to a Form ARB1FS/CS. (ARB1FS is for financial matters and ARB1CS is for children proceedings). If both of the couple are committed to achieving resolution, why would they not want to be contractually bound to have an adjudication if negotiation proves inconclusive. Whilst a blank refusal to do so might highlight a reason for issuing Form A or Form C100, in most cases, and particularly if fully explained, arbitration will be seen as preferable.

iii. The couple may have resolved most of the issues between them but have reached an impasse. Here give consideration to whether more specific guidance such as neutral evaluation is the way forward or, if absolute certainty and conclusion is required, the instruction of an arbitrator to finalise the outstanding points.

In all cases, the first step would be a precommitment meeting. Most arbitrators will facilitate this free of charge if the arbitration does not proceed. It is an opportunity to consider what might be required and how the arbitrator might be able to help.

Following the precommitment meeting, the couple will sign the ARB1FS/CS. This contractually binds them to the process. The arbitration will only not continue in the event that the arbitrator feels unable to continue working with the couple or both of them agree to be released from their contractual obligations.

Conventionally, a directions appointment will then be set. The couple with the assistance of their lawyers can agree directions which will then be approved by an arbitration the form of an award. Alternatively, directions may be imposed by the arbitrator.

If along the way, further assistance is required by the arbitrator, subsequent directions appointments can be arranged. Do note, however, that these might be separately charged outside of a cost quote provided for the arbitration itself. If the arbitration is to be by way of oral hearing, the costs quote will cover: -

- The precommitment meeting
- One directions appointment
- A one-day oral hearing (with subsequent days being separately charged)

- The provision of the award

The decision as to whether the arbitration will take place on paper or in person will usually be made either at the precommitment meeting or First Directions Appointment. This, of course, can, however, be changed if circumstances dictate this to be appropriate. A revision to the arbitrator's fees may take place at that stage.

If one of the couple would prefer an oral hearing but the other prefers for matters to be dealt with on paper (perhaps for reasons of cost), it is likely that the arbitrator will err on the side of the request for an oral hearing, as it is very important that both of the couple feel that they have been heard. The ability within arbitration to deal with the issue of costs on an entirely bespoke basis does, however, mean that perhaps a cost adjustment could be made if this were felt to be reasonable in all of the circumstances., i.e. the party requesting the oral hearing might bear the additional cost.

An award will not be delivered until the arbitrator's fees have been met in full. If one of the parties refuses to pay those costs, the other can discharge the fees in full, with the necessary adjustment being made within the award itself. An award will usually be delivered promptly. The arbitrator will agree with the couple at the time of the hearing or, if the arbitration is to be on paper, at the time of delivery of those papers when that award will be produced.

The award will be circulated simultaneously to all parties.

The award will then be converted into an order by consent for submission to the court by the lawyers instructed.

In children cases, the "award" is a "determination" and does not need to be submitted to the court, except perhaps in circumstances where subsequently one of the parents fails to adhere to the terms and the other may look to the court for enforcement. In such circumstances, however, a preferable route is to ascertain why adherence to the determination has not taken place. A discussion through a more communicative out of court method, such as mediation, would be the preferred step. It can be hugely beneficial to incorporate within any agreement arising from a determination an agreement to return to mediation or arbitration, should issues arise in the future. Similarly, this should be incorporated within a consent order in financial matters.

So, what are the concerns?

1. How do you choose your arbitrator?

   The selection of the arbitrator can be achieved in exactly the same way as the selection of the pFDR Judge. Again, it is always a good idea to involve the couple in the selection. It is useful to build your own directory of arbitrators whom you consider to be particularly suitable to a certain type of case. It can be handy to regularly update yourself in relation to fees. Liaise with the other side to see if you can mutually agree a group of six possible arbitrators with whom you are both content. Again, let one of the couple reduce the group to three and the other make the final decision. If you sense that one of the couple needs to feel "in control" let them have the "final word". It is important for people who need to feel in control to be allowed to be so in a situation where it doesn't matter. This is one of those. Similarly, if one of the couple is unrepresented allow them to make the final selection. This will produce far more inclusivity and can only assist the process.

2. Full and frank disclosure

   It is a common misconception among the public that the court process forces compliance – particularly with disclosure. Actually, an arbitrator who can talk directly to the couple at a pre-commitment or directions appointment is far more likely to encourage clear disclosure than any court order ever can.

Let's look at the case of Graham and Sally.

Graham and Sally had married in 1994 and separated in 2019. They have one adult son who lives independently. Both are working and have sufficient income to meet their needs. Sally continues to reside in the family home. She recognises that the property will need to be sold. Graham lives in rented accommodation.

Graham has been dealing with matters himself. He doesn't want to waste money on lawyers. He thinks that everything is quite straight forward. Sally has instructed a solicitor and Forms E have been engaged voluntarily. Graham started a new job in 2020. Sally believes that he will have a workplace pension with his new employment, but it is not referred to in his Form E. Her solicitor raises this with Graham who confirms that he does have a new pension but as this started after he and Sally separated, he is not disclosing it.

Sally wants to move on with her life. She wants to sell the family home. Although not living in the property, Graham refuses to do so until everything is sorted out including the pension.

Sally's solicitor tells Sally that she will have to issue Court proceedings if she wants matters resolved. Interestingly, Sally's solicitor does not consider neutral evaluation with her client as this is a process with which she is unfamiliar. She refers Sally for a MIAM. The accredited mediator discusses mediation. He, too, fails to mention neutral evaluation. Sally doesn't think mediation will work because Graham is fixated about not disclosing his new pension. The mediator suggests arbitration and explains that a pre-commitment meeting with an arbitrator will be free of charge if she and Graham decide not to proceed. Sally thinks this might appeal to Graham and asks her solicitor to write to him suggesting the process. Her solicitor does so and also includes a list of three possible arbitrators suggesting that Graham choose one of them.

Graham is attracted by the fact that the pre-commitment meeting is free of charge and so agrees. He hopes the arbitrator will tell Sally how unreasonable she is.

The pre-commitment meeting is arranged. The arbitrator is appraised of the issues and the problems with disclosure. At the pre-commitment meeting, the arbitrator explains to Graham that just because he provides the detail of his new pension does not mean it will be divided between himself and Sally. The arbitrator explains that she may decide it is a post-separation resource which should not be touched but explains to Graham that she cannot do her job properly if she does not know the full extent of the assets available between himself and Sally. Reassured by the fact that Sally may not actually receive anything from his pension, Graham provides full details.

The case settles with a sale of the family home and an equal division of the net proceeds. There is also to be an equal division of pension value excluding the new workplace pension which Graham will retain. Both are relieved. An award by consent is prepared. Sally's costs of the arbitration including drafting the consent order are £3,500 + VAT. The arbitrator's fee is £1,000 + VAT. Graham's costs are simply 50% of the arbitrator's fee i.e., £600.

Could matters have been dealt with differently?

An alternative option for Sally's solicitor might have been neutral evaluation as opposed to arbitration. The neutral evaluator provides a view. The arbitrator makes a decision. A neutral evaluation could have had the same effect. The subject of the neutral evaluation would have been a very narrow issue. In the case of Graham and Sally, the pre-commitment meeting with the arbitrator has achieved the same outcome.

It is unlikely that a Judge in the court process could have had such a candid conversation with Graham. The formality of the court process may have prevented this. One of the principal differences between a court-based Judge and a jointly appointed arbitrator is that the couple have the sense that the arbitrator, whom they have selected, is working with and for them both, having been charged with the task of making a decision. The Judge in the court system is state appointed. Their identity will not be known until either the day before or even the day of the hearing itself. Whilst of course they have a duty of care to the couple, what is missing is that extra bonding which arises in circumstances where specific selection followed by joint instruction is involved. This is a vitally important difference. What it also achieves is, following a decision, a recognition that although perhaps the decision was not what was hoped for, it was fairly and diligently imposed. Where one of the couple is on the receiving end of an outcome which they really don't like in the court process, it is only too easy to reach the conclusion that the Judge got it wrong. This can have a devastating impact on the family moving forwards as resentment can be difficult to remove. Those couples who find themselves in need of an adjudication are often either high conflict or have complex issues. There can of course simply be those who have insufficient to go around which makes division of resources very difficult. In each of these circumstances emotions may be high or hostility intense. Working with a jointly appointed adjudicator in whom trust has been placed can go a long way to eradicating this moving forwards. In circumstances where a couple continue to co-parent children long after lawyers have stepped aside, anything which can improve the relationship between those parents must be of benefit.

3. What happens if one party fails to comply with their obligations under the directions award?

We all know how difficult it can be to achieve compliance within the court process where one of the couple resolutely refuses to adhere to their obligations. Of course, it is possible to make application for a penal notice. Due to the inordinate delay within the court process, it can take many weeks for this to be dealt with. It is entirely usual for the dilatory party to comply shortly before an allocated court date for consideration is reached. This will then make it not cost effective to go to court simply to argue over the issue of costs. What a complete waste of time and money.

If, within the arbitration process, someone does not do what they should do, the arbitrator can be asked to convene a further directions appointment. The purpose will be to ascertain whether the delay in reasonable or whether one of the couple is simply being obdurate. The arbitrator will have a conversation and explain the cost risks of their approach. This direct involvement from the person who has been jointly instructed to undertake this task is infinitely more likely to have an effect than any application for a penal notice. The approach of the arbitrator will be massively more constructive. This neutrally appointed adjudicator can find out clearly why compliance has not taken place. There may be entirely good reason which has somehow been miscommunicated between the couple. If, however, there is no good reason, a suitably stern approach could be taken without the (futile) suggestion of imprisonment.

If assurances are given which are still not complied with, a further appointment can be arranged. The arbitrator can ensure that the party occasioning this extra work will meet the cost if appropriate. A dialogue is maintained. The arbitrator remains in close control of the process, which is hugely important. There is no opportunity for "drift". There is always a direct point of communication.

4. What happens if one party thinks that the outcome is unfair?

There is now the opportunity to appeal an arbitral award.

Whether or not the award of an arbitrator can be appealed has consistently been a source of concern for those solicitors contemplating a referral into arbitration. In *Haley v Haley [2020] EWCA Civ 1369* the Court of Appeal in financial remedy proceedings confirmed that a challenge to an arbitration award is not confined to the limited grounds set out in the Arbitration Act 1996 and the court has an independent, statutory duty to survey the fairness of any financial remedies order which sought to implement the arbitral award.

There followed the case of *G v G [2022] EWFC 151* which case concerned an application by the mother for permission to relocate form the West Country to London and for a child arrangements order. The parties agreed to attend arbitration. Following a two-day hearing, the appointed arbitrator delivered a determination on 12th August 2022, refusing the application to relocate and providing for a shared care arrangement. The mother sought to set aside the determination and hold a rehearing. The matter was transferred to the High Court and considered by Peel J. The principles already set out in *Haley v Haley* were considered. Peel J ruled that the same principles apply. "A judge being invited to make any welfare order under the Children Act 1989 must be independently satisfied that it is a proper order to make, the paramount consideration being the welfare of the child under section 1 (1) thereof" (paragraph 14).

This hopefully provides the reassurance sought by those who were initially wary of referring cases which might otherwise litigate into the process of arbitration.

But what if one of the couple simply does not like the outcome. They may to refuse to submit a consent order to the court. Notwithstanding the fact that they have become contractually bound to adhere to the arbitrator's decision, they may simply not be prepared to do so.

If this situation arises, a "notice to show cause" application will need to be made by the other party. The same criteria will be applied as would be the case in any similar situation where one of the couple was asserting agreement.

The first step is to ascertain whether there was an agreement. If Form ARB1 has been signed and the arbitrator has made a decision, then clearly there was an agreement. The issue then is whether the award was fair. This is something which may need to be determined within the court system. Costs will of course be an issue.

Due to the "buy in" by the couple to both the arbitrator and the process, hopefully this is something which might arise in only a handful of cases. Let's look at the case study of Lynne and Greg.

Lynne and Greg met in 2001. Neither wanted to marry. Lynne's parents had gone through a bitter divorce. Both of Greg's parents had died three years before in a horrific car accident. Greg, as an only child, had inherited the totality of their wealth, which was not insignificant.

Lynne and Greg went on to have three children in relatively quick succession. Greg was conscious of the fact that Lynne felt unprotected. They lived in a home which was in Greg's sole name. One of Lynne's friends had recently separated from her cohabitee partner and had found herself in the invidious position of having to move into rented accommodation. She had one child. Her former partner refused to pay any form of maintenance, so she had to make application to the Child Maintenance Service. She found herself with insufficient funds and was in an extremely invidious position. This made Lynne understandably nervous. Greg recognised this. He suggested that they enter into a cohabitation agreement, which would provide for Lynne in the event of separation. Lynne and Greg instructed separate solicitors. Greg covered the cost of the legal advice. Lynne felt comforted.

Lynne and Greg then decided that they did want to marry. They had been together now for over ten years. Greg had been advised when the cohabitation agreement had been prepared that were he ever to marry in the future it would be sensible to enter into a mirror prenuptial agreement. The cohabitation agreement referred to this.

Greg and Lynne went back to their previous solicitors. The prenuptial agreement was intended to protect Greg in the event that the marriage broke down in its early stages. Lynne was to receive sufficient from the available resources to rehouse herself and the children. Greg recognised that the longer the marriage continued, the more Lynne was giving up by entering into this agreement. It was therefore proposed that Lynne should receive in addition to the costs of accommodation a lump sum which would increase by percentage on a year-by-year basis.

The prenuptial agreement included provision for a review every five years. Greg and Lynne simply forgot to take advantage of this.

As is often the case, the assumption of Greg and Lynne was that if their marriage continued for a long time, it was unlikely that they would separate and therefore reference would not need to be made to the prenuptial agreement.

Very sadly, after having been together for over twenty years, Greg met and fell hopelessly in love with Sophie. Lynne was devastated. Lynne was angry. Lynne was absorbed with grief. Greg was sad but resolute that their relationship was over.

Lynne took advice. Reference was made to the cohabitation and prenuptial agreements. Over the years, Greg and Lynne had spent a great deal and their "pot" had reduced. The percentage increase to the lump sum which had been provided for Lynne actually meant that the sum which she would receive from their joint resources would leave Greg with very little. Arguably, he would have insufficient funds to meet the cost of suitable future accommodation. Lynne was rather pleased about this. Greg could not see how this could be fair. The prenuptial agreement was intended to protect his wealth. It now appeared to have completely the reverse effect. Both had taken proper legal advice at the time the prenuptial agreement had been drafted. Lynne pointed out that he was the one who had suggested the agreement. He should now stand by its terms.

Although reviews had not taken place, the prenuptial agreement confirmed that in the absence of alteration the agreement would stand.

The matter went to arbitration.

Lynne was content for the matter to be dealt with on paper. She felt that the prenuptial agreement was entirely clear and should be upheld. It had taken matters a stage further from the cohabitation agreement due to the longevity of their relationship. Lynne had been advised that the only ground upon which the prenuptial agreement might be set aside was as a consequence of the financial situation which Greg would be left in and whether that were fair. Lynne retorted that Greg was living with Sophie now. Sophie has her own home. Greg has a substantial income and some capital.

Greg wanted the matter to be dealt with orally as he felt evidence would be important. At the precommitment meeting, the arbitrator's view was that there should be an oral hearing. Greg volunteered to pay the difference in cost between an "on paper" hearing and an oral hearing. Lynne was content with this.

After a one-day final hearing, the arbitrator's decision was that the outcome occasioned by the prenuptial agreement was so manifestly unfair to Greg that it could not be upheld. Greg would be left with only a very small deposit. Even with his mortgage capacity, he would struggle to provide suitable accommodation for himself. A different capital division was imposed. The capital division was not necessarily in line with that which a Court would order were there no prenuptial agreement but was sufficient to meet Greg's reasonable capital needs in terms of the provision of accommodation.

Lynne was incensed. She refused to agree to the consent order being lodged with the court. Greg struggled with how this could be the case. Surely Lynne had committed to the arbitration process. She now seemed to say that she would not adhere to the decision made.

Greg was advised to make application for notice to show cause. He was troubled by the additional cost which now was going to be incurred and the inevitable delay of the court process. Matters were listed more swiftly than he envisaged.

The court upheld the award produced by the arbitrator. A court order was made. Although Greg would have been entitled to make application for his costs, his decision was not to do so. He recognised that Lynne had been extremely upset. She was, after all, the mother of his children and he hoped that something of their relationship could be salvaged.

Lynne wrote to the arbitrator setting out at some length how unfair she felt the process to have been.

The arbitrator, not wishing to engage in any correspondence following delivery of the award with either of the parties, simply acknowledged receipt.

Lynne immediately expressed her gratitude that her communication had been read. She acknowledged that there was nothing which she could do and appeared to understand that the outcome overall was fair. It appeared that satisfactory conclusion had been achieved.

The situation of Lynne and Greg is a rather extreme version of events but shows how such situations would be handled within the arbitration process. The same would apply in any situation where either party felt aggrieved by the award made, notwithstanding the fact that their legal advice was that the outcome was within the bracket of that which a court would award.

5. What if both parties are unrepresented?

In a world where legal fees are becoming increasingly unaffordable and public funding remains unavailable in almost all situations, there is the increasing likelihood that separating couples who feel they simply need the assistance of someone who can give an adjudication may "self-refer" to arbitration.

In cases where resources are limited, this may be a sensible solution. If the parties are able, in clear terms, to set out the available assets the arbitrator may be able to reach a decision.

There may, however, be circumstances where a couple with complex financial circumstances may seek to short circuit the legal process and avoid costs. There is a risk that this may place the arbitrator in an invidious position. It is open to the arbitrator at a precommitment meeting to decline to accept the instructions and the arbitrator should not be afraid to do so if they feel that the task placed before them is unreasonable or untenable.

Similarly, whilst an arbitrator can provide direction and information, they cannot provide advice. It is essential that, at all times, professional boundaries are maintained. This will be a judgment call for the arbitrator.

What may become more commonplace is the referral into arbitration by a mediator of an unrepresented couple who have been unable to resolve all issues in the mediation process.

Take the example of Jack and Sam.

Jack and Sam initially entered into a civil partnership and subsequently married.

Jack works as a postman. Sam is a manager at a local supermarket. Both have pension provision, although Sam's is more valuable. Sam also has a higher income than Jack and consequentially a higher mortgage capacity.

The deposit for the family home which is held in joint names through inheritance from his grandparents. Throughout the relationship, Sam has discharged the mortgage. Bills have been shared. Jack has paid for what they describe as "extras", including the hire purchase on their Kia motor vehicle, which is in Jack's name.

Sam could be described as the "leaver" in the relationship. He had recently joined a cycling club and had acquired a circle of friends with whom Jack did not really feel comfortable. This began to drive a wedge between them. Sam's expectation was that they would simply separate; that he would recover the funds which he had invested in the family home, the uplift in value being divided between himself and Jack. He felt that his interest in the car should be offset against Jack's interest in the uplift in value of the home and that they would each keep their own pensions.

Jack was understandably upset by the breakdown of the relationship. He had no wish to engage in any form of acrimonious discussion with Sam. He knew that they had to separate, and his expectation was that Sam would buy him out of the family home. As a consequence of the encouragement of his friends and family, however, Jack ascertained that perhaps Sam's approach to the division of their joint wealth was a little one sided. Keen to remain as amicable as possible, Jack suggested the process of mediation. Sam saw this as unnecessary but, still feeling guilty and keen to get matters resolved, agreed.

Jack and Sam engaged in mediation with Alex. Alex provided each of them with a Form E to complete and exchange on a voluntary basis. Alex then prepared an asset schedule for simplicity of consideration.

Jack and Sam were content to accept that there should be a clean break between them, notwithstanding the disparity in income. Sam also conceded that it would be reasonable for there to be a pension sharing order equalising the respective pension provision.

Sam was also content for Jack to retain the Kia motor vehicle, but it was on the basis that he would recover his investment in the family home and only any uplift would be shared.

Jack's position was as he had the lower mortgage capacity, he had a greater need for capital in order to rehouse and that he was only content to agree to a clean break if he had adequate financial provision. He would be prepared to offset 50% of the value of the car but only if the net proceeds of sale of the house were divided between them equally. He was prepared for Sam to buy him out of the property if that were achievable, but he was not prepared to budge on his position.

After three mediation sessions, Jack and Sam conceded that they had reached an impasse. Alex discussed whether a neutral evaluator may be able to assist. In particular, Jack's concern was that this would not be inexpensive and might not be conclusive. Jack and Sam's joint preference was to refer the matter to an arbitrator for an "on paper" decision.

Alex prepared a note for the arbitrator, which was accompanied by the agreed asset schedule. The note explained the background of the situation of Jack and Sam with clear details of their personal and financial circumstances.

Alex set out that which was agreed between Jack and Sam.

Alex also prepared a Form ARB1FS, which set out the issues to be decided, i.e.

i. The division of the value/proceeds of sale of the family home

ii. The treatment of the value of the car

The joint instructions were approved by both Jack and Sam. Both were given the opportunity to take independent legal advice. They both declined to do so, and this was recorded by Alex.

Jack and Sam attended a precommitment meeting with the arbitrator. The arbitrator confirmed that they were content to take on the arbitration and confirmed that a paper exercise would be sufficient.

The arbitrator did not see a need for a separate directions appointment but provided a directions award requiring both Jack and Sam to prepare a written statement setting out their respective positions. The arbitrator also directed that each should obtain a mortgage capacity report and provide property particulars which they felt would be suitable for themselves and the other.

A date for submission of statements was set.

The decision made is not relevant, save to say that resolution was achieved. The arbitrator's fees, paid in full before the written award was delivered, were acceptable to both Jack and Sam. Both felt that their case had been listened to and fully considered. Both had agreed to abide by the decision of the arbitrator.

Alex, a solicitor as well as a mediator, had agreed to prepare on a joint instruction basis a consent order arising from the award provided. Had Alex not been prepared to do so, Jack and Sam would have needed to find a cost-effective way to have this piece of work undertaken. With the advent of "one lawyer one couple" such facility would be easy for them to achieve.

At every important stage, Jack and Sam were offered the opportunity to take independent legal advice. Whether they did so was a matter for them. The mediator had used their skill to try to assist them to reach an agreed outcome. This has been achieved but only in part. A decision had to be made on the two remaining issues. The arbitrator felt content to undertake this at a relatively low-cost level. Although, inevitably, costs had been incurred, those costs were both modest and manageable for Jack and Sam.

6. The Reluctant Participant/No Desire for Outcome

Much has been said about the separating spouse who has no wish to resolve matters but rather prefers to maintain what can be described as toxic contact with the other party and perpetuate drama and chaos. Such individuals may see any form of out of court dispute resolution as an opportunity to prolong the process and incur unnecessary legal cost for the other party.

Of course, there are also those who simply don't want the relationship to come to an end and will therefore do everything possible to avoid resolution as such resolution can only mean the complete termination of a relationship which they hope to hang on to. Any form of ongoing communication is better than nothing.

Family law professionals understand that whatever the motivation, it is better for both of the couple to move on with their lives, as to remain in any form of ongoing dispute can never be beneficial, especially not for any children. This can be the position whether the children are in their minority or adults.

In either circumstance, the use of arbitration as an ultimate determining process can be hugely beneficial.

Take the example of Ruth and Jack:-

Ruth and Jack have been married for 38 years. They have three adult children respectively aged 31, 34 and 36. Both are now aged 65. Ruth had the expectation of spending more time with the family and, in particular, her grandchildren. Following the death of Jack's parents, he had inherited a holiday home in North Wales. Ruth anticipated spending holiday time there with the family. She also hoped that she and Jack might travel more extensively than they had been able to do while they were both working.

Jack has formed a new relationship with a widow, Sharon, who has been known to Ruth and Jack for some considerable time (their middle son was at school with Sharon's daughter). For a long time, Jack has been disillusioned with his relationship with Ruth but was too involved in both work and other matters to properly address the situation.

He and Sharon met by accident at Gatwick Airport when they both happened to be stuck there with flights delayed. Jack was travelling for business whereas Sharon was on her way to spend a few days with a girlfriend.

Jack realised that his relationship with Sharon was likely to become permanent. He informed Ruth of his decision, knowing that doing so was going to be beyond difficult. Ruth's reaction was as expected. She was hurt, angry, vengeful, disappointed and distraught.

Ever pragmatic, Jack simply wanted to get on with things. Now that "no fault" divorce was available to hm, he issued a divorce application having first offered Ruth the opportunity to do so. Unfortunately, she did not get on with things as quickly as Jack had hoped. He simply wanted everything to be over with so that he could move on with his life. Ruth had a very different approach to the situation.

Ruth's failure to engage in the process caused Jack to contact an accredited mediator with a view to Form FM1 being signed, enabling him to lodge Form A with the court and get on with things. Ruth, however, told the mediator that she would be interested in mediation. She hoped that this might give her the opportunity to drag things out. She remained ever optimistic that Jack might come to his senses.

Jack's solicitor advised him against turning down the opportunity to mediate. Jack had no objection to engaging in the mediation process but was nervous that Ruth would see this as simply an opportunity to prolong matters. It was therefore put to Ruth that Jack would only engage in mediation if Ruth were prepared in advance to sign ARB1FS, thereby committing her to the arbitration process in the event that mediation did not work. Whilst this did not accord with Ruth's approach, she found herself in a difficult position. If she failed to agree, Jack was likely to go ahead with the court process. If, however, she accepted this condition, matters were likely to be resolved far more quicky than she would hope.

This approach, whilst unattractive for Ruth, is probably the best way forward for both Jack and Ruth. If Jack is determined to end the relationship, there is nothing to be gained by Ruth by continuing conflict, as this is likely to further erode an already very damaged relationship. Jack simply wants things to be over with. The facility of mediation followed, if necessary, by arbitration provides Jack and Ruth with a forum within which to discuss and hopefully resolve the issues which exist between them in a manner which just might also create a better ongoing relationship between them for the benefit of their three adult children. If they absolutely cannot agree, they will work together with a jointly selected arbitrator which has a far more inclusive feeling to it than the imposition of an outcome by an unidentified member of the judiciary.

> If, as opposed to being angry and hurt, Ruth had more Machiavellian reasons for wanting to avoid resolution, the same methodology would apply and should be put in place by the lawyers involved.
>
> Let's say Ruth had been the person instigating Form A and thereby first meeting with the accredited mediator. She might ask simply for Form FM1 to be signed. The mediator does, however, have an obligation to contact Jack and if Jack is minded to engage in the mediation process the couple ought to be steered by the family law professionals into an out of court dispute resolution method.

If mediation seems unlikely to work ahead of the proposed arbitration, a private FDR is always an alternative option, or a neutral evaluation. As indicated previously, all of these out of court methods are interlinked and interchangeable. If you believe that "the other side" may simply be prevaricating by proposing either neutral evaluation, mediation or a private FDR, you might want to suggest that a condition of engaging in such process is to have the Form ARB1 signed in advance, so that in the event that a discursive method does not achieve resolution, the final backstop of a possible out of court adjudication is already in place.

CHAPTER THIRTEEN

THE CERTAINTY PROJECT

The Certainty Project represents the fusion of an ability to create an outcome but if you are unable to do so, to have an adjudication. The title "Certainty Project" derives from the idea that separating couples seek as much "certainty" as can be achieved at the conclusion of a relationship. This applies to certainty of timing, location, cost and outcome.

The project can be applied to both financial remedy and children proceedings. The intention is that both parties will be represented bit it can apply equally well to litigants in person. An arbitrator will be selected to have overall "umbrella" control of the process and ARB1FS/CS will be signed. First, however, the couple will engage in the process of mediation, their solicitors if instructed having first dealt with the issue of disclosure.

The mediator will endeavour to assist the couple in reaching resolution. If the couple prefer, they might engage in the collaborative approach as opposed to mediation. Mediation can be either classic or hybrid.

Other methods of dispute resolution can also be considered. Neutral evaluation may be of assistance or, similarly, a private FDR.

If the couple are able to achieve resolution through a discursive process, the arbitrator will simply prepare an award/determination by consent. If some but not all issues are resolved, the arbitrator will make a decision in relation to those outstanding. If the couple have been unable to agree on anything, they will move into the arbitration process.

The certainty of cost derives from an ability to provide a costs quote at the outset for the most probable scenario, i.e., a decision through arbitration. The couple then know that if they are able to achieve resolution at an earlier stage, there is a cost saving to be made.

In term of certainty of timing, process is able to dovetail with the 20-week window between issue of a divorce application and pronouncement of conditional order, thereby ensuring that a uniformity of overall time frame is achievable.

For those who like structure within an otherwise bespoke service The Certainty Project, as a method of working, can provide exactly that. Details of practitioners who are willing to engage in The Certainty Project can be found on The Certainty Project website.

So, let's look at how this works in practice: -

After many years of feeling trapped in a toxic and potentially coercive relationship, Sarah finds the courage to end her relationship with Ian. They have three sons who are aged 19, 17 and 14. Ian is outraged. Continued joint occupancy of the family home is tense. Sarah needs to resolve matters as expeditiously as she can. She has limited resources. Her parents have offered to assist her with legal fees.

Sarah takes legal advice. Her solicitor recommends The Certainty Project. Sarah believes that Ian is more likely to engage in a process which he believes to be innovative and cost effective. It will also help if he feels in control.

In an initial communication from Sarah's solicitor, The Certainty Project is proposed. Ian in invited to select an arbitrator. He is also invited to select a mediator.

Form ARB1FS is prepared, signed and circulated. Both solicitors provide a cost estimate to their respective clients based upon the matter going through mediation unsuccessfully and then requiring a decision via the process of arbitration. This cost estimate does not include the costs of the mediator but will include the "worst case scenario" costs for the arbitrator, which will have been settled at the time of the arbitrator's appointment.

Sarah's preference is to engage in hybrid mediation. She wants the opportunity to discuss matters in confidence with the mediator. Sarah would like to be supported by her lawyer in the mediation sessions. Ian sees this as unnecessary.

Both Sarah and Ian arrange an intake session with the mediator. The mediator explains that how they wish to be supported through the mediation process is a matter for each of them, but part of the mediator's role is to ensure a "level playing field" at all times. Ian will not therefore be disadvantaged if he chooses not to have his lawyer present with hm in the sessions. He decides that having them available by telephone if required is his ideal and cost-effective solution.

Sarah's preference is, if possible, to retain the family home but to offset her interest in Ian's pension. Due to lack of agreement in relation to valuation, a single joint expert needs to be instructed to deal with the value of the family home and also a pension report is required. Sarah and Ian are unable to agree on the wording of each letter of joint instruction. By email the arbitrator is asked to adjudicate over this interim issue. This is handled swiftly within a matter of days. Sarah and Ian are contractually bound to abide by the arbitrator's decision.

If Sarah and Ian are able to resolve all issues without further involvement of the arbitrator, an award by consent will be prepared. If they are only able to resolve a number of issues (or, indeed, nothing at all), they will move to a directions appointment with their arbitrator. The process then follows the usual pattern. Also remember, however, that you can specifically tailor that pattern to the actual requirements of the couple.

AND FINALLY…

TOP TIPS FOR OUT OF COURT DISPUTE RESOLUTION

Hopefully, you have now reached the conclusion that almost all issues can be resolved "out of court". You have developed a familiarity with the various processes which might be available. You feel confident to recommend these processes to your clients. You recognise that in doing so you can still maintain a profitable practice.

So, what are the key points to remember?

1. Your new client may have an expectation that the court system will provide them with "retribution and justice". You know that this is unlikely to be the case. Before issuing any form of court application, ask yourself what your client hopes to achieve and why. What are the alternatives which you might consider? Your court application should be an absolute last resort and even if issued you will want to consider alternative methods of dispute resolution alongside the process which might result in a stay or could achieve an outcome in advance of the first allocated appointment.

2. Dispute resolution methods really are "alternatives". This is not "one size fits all". Consider the various options available and what would best suit the individual needs of your client.

3. Build yourself a list of preferred practitioners for each of the options which you would wish to consider.

4. Ensure that you cannot be perceived to be the "belligerent other side" who refuses to consider options other than court.

5. Make sure that you/other members of your team can offer out of court dispute resolution methods. Whilst specific training is required to meditate or arbitrate, or to engage in collaborative practice, only the appropriate level of competence is required to provide a neutral evaluation or act as a pFDR judge.

6. Practise your powers of persuasion on "the other side", who probably do not want to be perceived as being firmly fixed in the past so far as dispute resolution methods are concerned or unwilling to embrace cost and time efficient alternative options which can only be of benefit to their client.

7. Out of court dispute resolution options are entirely bespoke. Have the confidence to build the dispute resolution method which provides your client and their family with time and cost-efficient options to bring their relationship to a satisfactory conclusion.

MORE BOOKS BY LAW BRIEF PUBLISHING

A selection of our other titles available now:-

'A Practical Guide to Parental Alienation in Private and Public Law Children Cases' by Sam King QC & Frankie Shama
'Contested Heritage – Removing Art from Land and Historic Buildings' by Richard Harwood QC, Catherine Dobson, David Sawtell
'The Limits of Separate Legal Personality: When Those Running a Company Can Be Held Personally Liable for Losses Caused to Third Parties Outside of the Company' by Dr Mike Wilkinson
'A Practical Guide to Transgender Law' by Robin Moira White & Nicola Newbegin
'Artificial Intelligence – The Practical Legal Issues (2nd Edition)' by John Buyers
'A Practical Guide to Residential Freehold Conveyancing' by Lorraine Richardson
'A Practical Guide to Pensions on Divorce for Lawyers' by Bryan Scant
'A Practical Guide to Challenging Sham Marriage Allegations in Immigration Law' by Priya Solanki
'A Practical Guide to Legal Rights in Scotland' by Sarah-Jane Macdonald
'A Practical Guide to New Build Conveyancing' by Paul Sams & Rebecca East
'A Practical Guide to Defending Barristers in Disciplinary Cases' by Marc Beaumont
'A Practical Guide to Inherited Wealth on Divorce' by Hayley Trim
'A Practical Guide to Practice Direction 12J and Domestic Abuse in Private Law Children Proceedings' by Rebecca Cross & Malvika Jaganmohan
'A Practical Guide to Confiscation and Restraint' by Narita Bahra QC, John Carl Townsend, David Winch
'A Practical Guide to the Law of Forests in Scotland' by Philip Buchan
'A Practical Guide to Health and Medical Cases in Immigration Law' by Rebecca Chapman & Miranda Butler
'A Practical Guide to Bad Character Evidence for Criminal Practitioners by Aparna Rao
'A Practical Guide to Extradition Law post-Brexit' by Myles Grandison et al

'A Practical Guide to Hoarding and Mental Health for Housing Lawyers' by Rachel Coyle
'A Practical Guide to Psychiatric Claims in Personal Injury – 2nd Edition' by Liam Ryan
'Stephens on Contractual Indemnities' by Richard Stephens
'A Practical Guide to the EU Succession Regulation' by Richard Frimston
'A Practical Guide to Solicitor and Client Costs – 2nd Edition' by Robin Dunne
'Constructive Dismissal – Practice Pointers and Principles' by Benjimin Burgher
'A Practical Guide to Religion and Belief Discrimination Claims in the Workplace' by Kashif Ali
'A Practical Guide to the Law of Medical Treatment Decisions' by Ben Troke
'Fundamental Dishonesty and QOCS in Personal Injury Proceedings: Law and Practice' by Jake Rowley
'A Practical Guide to the Law in Relation to School Exclusions' by Charlotte Hadfield & Alice de Coverley
'A Practical Guide to Divorce for the Silver Separators' by Karin Walker
'The Right to be Forgotten – The Law and Practical Issues' by Melissa Stock
'A Practical Guide to Planning Law and Rights of Way in National Parks, the Broads and AONBs' by James Maurici QC, James Neill et al
'A Practical Guide to Election Law' by Tom Tabori
'A Practical Guide to the Law in Relation to Surrogacy' by Andrew Powell
'A Practical Guide to Claims Arising from Fatal Accidents – 2nd Edition' by James Patience
'A Practical Guide to the Ownership of Employee Inventions – From Entitlement to Compensation' by James Tumbridge & Ashley Roughton
'A Practical Guide to Asbestos Claims' by Jonathan Owen & Gareth McAloon
'A Practical Guide to Stamp Duty Land Tax in England and Northern Ireland' by Suzanne O'Hara
'A Practical Guide to the Law of Farming Partnerships' by Philip Whitcomb
'Covid-19, Homeworking and the Law – The Essential Guide to Employment and GDPR Issues' by Forbes Solicitors
'Covid-19 and Criminal Law – The Essential Guide' by Ramya Nagesh
'Covid-19 and Family Law in England and Wales – The Essential Guide' by Safda Mahmood

‘A Practical Guide to the Law of Unlawful Eviction and Harassment – 2nd Edition’ by Stephanie Lovegrove
‘Covid-19, Brexit and the Law of Commercial Leases – The Essential Guide’ by Mark Shelton
‘A Practical Guide to Costs in Personal Injury Claims – 2nd Edition’ by Matthew Hoe
‘A Practical Guide to the General Data Protection Regulation (GDPR) – 2nd Edition’ by Keith Markham
‘Ellis on Credit Hire – Sixth Edition’ by Aidan Ellis & Tim Kevan
‘A Practical Guide to Working with Litigants in Person and McKenzie Friends in Family Cases’ by Stuart Barlow
‘Protecting Unregistered Brands: A Practical Guide to the Law of Passing Off’ by Lorna Brazell
‘A Practical Guide to Secondary Liability and Joint Enterprise Post-Jogee’ by Joanne Cecil & James Mehigan
‘A Practical Guide to the Pre-Action RTA Claims Protocol for Personal Injury Lawyers’ by Antonia Ford
‘A Practical Guide to Neighbour Disputes and the Law’ by Alexander Walsh
‘A Practical Guide to Forfeiture of Leases’ by Mark Shelton
‘A Practical Guide to Coercive Control for Legal Practitioners and Victims’ by Rachel Horman
‘A Practical Guide to Rights Over Airspace and Subsoil’ by Daniel Gatty
‘Tackling Disclosure in the Criminal Courts – A Practitioner’s Guide’ by Narita Bahra QC & Don Ramble
‘A Practical Guide to the Law of Driverless Cars – Second Edition’ by Alex Glassbrook, Emma Northey & Scarlett Milligan
‘A Practical Guide to TOLATA Claims’ by Greg Williams
‘A Practical Guide to Elderly Law – 2nd Edition’ by Justin Patten
‘A Practical Guide to Responding to Housing Disrepair and Unfitness Claims’ by Iain Wightwick
‘A Practical Guide to the Construction and Rectification of Wills and Trust Instruments’ by Edward Hewitt
‘A Practical Guide to the Law of Bullying and Harassment in the Workplace’ by Philip Hyland
‘How to Be a Freelance Solicitor: A Practical Guide to the SRA-Regulated Freelance Solicitor Model’ by Paul Bennett

'A Practical Guide to Prison Injury Claims' by Malcolm Johnson
'A Practical Guide to the Small Claims Track - 2nd Edition' by Dominic Bright
'A Practical Guide to Advising Clients at the Police Station' by Colin Stephen McKeown-Beaumont
'A Practical Guide to Antisocial Behaviour Injunctions' by Iain Wightwick
'Practical Mediation: A Guide for Mediators, Advocates, Advisers, Lawyers, and Students in Civil, Commercial, Business, Property, Workplace, and Employment Cases' by Jonathan Dingle with John Sephton
'The Mini-Pupillage Workbook' by David Boyle
'A Practical Guide to Crofting Law' by Brian Inkster
'A Practical Guide to Spousal Maintenance' by Liz Cowell
'A Practical Guide to the Law of Domain Names and Cybersquatting' by Andrew Clemson
'A Practical Guide to the Law of Gender Pay Gap Reporting' by Harini Iyengar
'A Practical Guide to the Rights of Grandparents in Children Proceedings' by Stuart Barlow
'NHS Whistleblowing and the Law' by Joseph England
'Employment Law and the Gig Economy' by Nigel Mackay & Annie Powell
'A Practical Guide to Noise Induced Hearing Loss (NIHL) Claims' by Andrew Mckie, Ian Skeate, Gareth McAloon
'An Introduction to Beauty Negligence Claims – A Practical Guide for the Personal Injury Practitioner' by Greg Almond
'Intercompany Agreements for Transfer Pricing Compliance' by Paul Sutton
'Zen and the Art of Mediation' by Martin Plowman
'A Practical Guide to the SRA Principles, Individual and Law Firm Codes of Conduct 2019 – What Every Law Firm Needs to Know' by Paul Bennett
'A Practical Guide to Adoption for Family Lawyers' by Graham Pegg
'A Practical Guide to Industrial Disease Claims' by Andrew Mckie & Ian Skeate
'A Practical Guide to Redundancy' by Philip Hyland
'A Practical Guide to Vicarious Liability' by Mariel Irvine
'A Practical Guide to Applications for Landlord's Consent and Variation of Leases' by Mark Shelton
'A Practical Guide to Relief from Sanctions Post-Mitchell and Denton' by Peter Causton

www.ingramcontent.com/pod-product-compliance
Lightning Source LLC
LaVergne TN
LVHW022117200926
848481LV00003B/1185
* 9 7 8 1 9 1 4 6 0 8 8 9 6 *